TELL ME THIS IS NORMAL

Julie O'Callaghan was born in Chicago in 1954, and has lived in Ireland since 1974. Her collections of poetry include *Edible Anecdotes* (Dolmen Press, 1983), a Poetry Book Society Recommendation; *What's What* (Bloodaxe Books, 1991), a Poetry Book Society Choice; and *No Can Do* (Bloodaxe Books, 2000), a Poetry Book Society Recommendation. *Tell Me This Is Normal: New & Selected Poems* (Bloodaxe Books, 2008) contains work from those three collections, together with newer poems, and is a Poetry Book Society Recommendation.

She has published poetry in many newspapers and journals, including *The Observer*, *The Guardian*, *The Times Literary Supplement*, *The Irish Times*, *Poetry Ireland Review* and *New Statesman*. She received the Michael Hartnett Poetry Award in 2001 and was awarded Arts Council of Ireland Bursaries in 1985, 1990 and 1998.

Her poems for older children have appeared in numerous anthologies in the UK (including the *New Oxford Book of Children's Verse* and *New Faber Book of Children's Verse*) and in school texts in Ireland, England, America and Canada. Her children's poems are collected in *Bright Lights Blaze Out* (Oxford University Press, 1986), *Cambridge Contemporary Poets 2* (Cambridge University Press, 1992), and in three full-length collections, *Taking My Pen for a Walk* (Orchard Books, 1988), *Two Barks* (Bloodaxe Books, 1998) and *The Book of Whispers* (Faber & Faber, 2006).

She is a member of the Irish academy of arts, Aosdána.

JULIE O'CALLAGHAN

TELL ME THIS IS NORMAL

NEW & SELECTED POEMS

BLOODAXE BOOKS

ISBN: 978 1 85224 790 4

First published 2008 by
Bloodaxe Books Ltd,
Highgreen,
Tarset,
Northumberland NE48 1RP.

www.bloodaxebooks.com
For further information about Bloodaxe titles
please visit our website or write to
the above address for a catalogue.

Bloodaxe Books Ltd acknowledges
the financial assistance of
Arts Council England, North East.

Cover design: Neil Astley & Pamela Robertson-Pearce.

Cover printing: J. Thomson Colour Printers Ltd, Glasgow.

Printed in Great Britain by
Bell & Bain Limited, Glasgow, Scotland.

for Dennis

ACKNOWLEDGEMENTS

This book includes poems selected from Julie O'Callaghan's collections *Edible Anecdotes* (Dolmen Press, 1983), *What's What* (Bloodaxe Books, 1991) and *No Can Do* (Bloodaxe Books, 2000), as well as a selection of new poems. The section entitled *Calligraphy* collects poems from her books which were inspired by *The Pillow Book of Sei Shonagon*.

Acknowledgements are due to the editors or producers of the following publications or programmes where some of the new poems first appeared: *BBC Poetry Proms*, *Oxford Magazine*, *Poetry Ireland Review*, *Portal*, *Sunday Miscellany* (RTE Radio 1), *The Irish Times* and *The Recorder*. Special thanks to William Corbett for *Problems* (Pressed Wafer, Boston, 2005).

CONTENTS

CALLIGRAPHY (1983–2000)

NEW POEMS (2008)

Edible Anecdotes

(1983)

EDIBLE ANECDOTES

Preamble

Mary Fran, Kathy, Lizzy,
my own dear cousins, for that you did
transport me to Dairy Queen
and there repeatedly force me
to eat hot fudge sundaes;
and also, that at your premises on Pratt Avenue
you did compel me to partake of
chocolate chip cookies
and brownies under false pretences.
You may be seated.
Jack and Rosemary, my misguided parents,
that you did, on numerous occasions,
lure me against my will into eating houses,
to wit, Poppin Fresh Pies, Town and Country,
The International Pancake House, Dunkin Donuts,
Mario's Italian Lemonade Stand, among others
and did wantonly thrust sundry items
of food in front of my face.
Next, please.
Kate, Ellen and Nora, siblings, you also
did cause me to procure Hostess Twinkies,
onion pizzas, popsicles,
Arby's Roast Beef sandwiches,
bagels and cream cheese.
The aforementioned are the principal
defendants in this case
but I must also indict my mouth
for aiding and abetting them
in the corruption of my body.
The court may rise.

Edible Anecdotes

1

I'm in this bookshop
with wooden floors and a great stereo
when this creep
standing at 'Vegetarian Cookbooks'
gives me a look
right out of some corny novel
so I mosey over to Women's Studies
open a copy of *Sisters United* and watch
as his goo-goo eyes
revert back to recipes
for soy bean casserole

2

stiff-legged, heavy-footed, dim-witted,
dry-mouthed and hang-dogged at three a.m.
we climb from the car
after seven hours driving
and shiver as we yawn
in front of Howard Johnson's Cafeteria
squinting from the bright lights
we sit at the counter
beside truck drivers eating apple pie
we wait for our toasted cheese sandwiches
and french fries listening to country western music
examining the bird life on our sugar packets

4

a building
made of steel and glass
just flew by overhead
some businessmen
were hanging out the windows
with party hats on
for a few minutes
I considered this to be
out of the ordinary
but on second thought
I continued
eating my sandwich

6

I drove out to the Casa del Sol Shopping Center
with the kids this morning
and in between the times when one of them
was grabbing bags of Hershey's Kisses
and insisting I buy them
and the other was poking his mitten
in the live lobster tank
I became depressed
and clutched something to renew my spirits:
Frozen Chocolate Cream Pie

7

a few things we keep in stock
like hands, arms, legs with high heels
then we've got the seasonal items such as
hearts, pine trees, turkeys, Uncle Sams, pumpkins,
maybe a Shakespeare's head or two
and sometimes Beethoven's
we've always got the touristy stuff
the Water Tower, John Hancock Building,
Civic Opera House, the mayor and the skyline
but the biggest demand is for individual pieces
some guy'll call us up and say
'I want my wife sculpted in dark chocolate
for our anniversary' – you know the type
a real eccentric
we take on all comers
the weirder the better
we like to think of our business
as edible art

9

Jimmy Dean stood outside a model Western saloon
signing autographs with diamond cuff links glittering
and pointy cowboy boots wishing they could vamoose
as we entered the Wisconsin State Fair
it was an iridescent midwestern day
so we rode the ferris wheel
screaming as we flew over the top
catching the breeze in our ears
I won a set of china ponies with feather manes

and we all sat down to free brochures
on pig feed and tractors
licking fudgicles and cotton candy

11

off in foreign climes
shovelling down my food
I could become a traitor
to the red white and blue
my plate covered with steam
I fill my fork
and swallow a mouthful
of peas potatoes and turnip:
green white orange

12

two girls
old enough to wear pantyhose
leaned against a green lamp post
eating fish and chips
from a piece of newspaper
one had yellow shoes
the other had white
the lamp post was on a gray brick street
which matched their eyes
it started raining
all I heard them say was
hurry up we'll miss the cartoons
the yellow shod girl
crumpled the paper
threw it in the gutter
two pairs of shoes
ran up the street

13

at about 3:30 on July 17th
just as the boredom
is thick and gooey
as salt water taffy
just as you watch
another mosquito on your wrist
sucking your blood

just as you've done all the things
you dreamt about in winter
three or four times
they will always suggest
setting up a lemonade stand
you go into the dark house
to see about the ice cubes

14

look at it this way, cookie
ya wanna make it big
or ya wanna spend the rest a yer life
playing bit parts in dog food commercials?
sweetheart, I know it ain't gonna be easy
but no one is gonna hire a two-ton-tessy
for their swanky prime-time serial
with designer wardrobe the way it costs
ya gotta cut out the Sara Lee Cheesecake
and the Pepperidge Farm Chocolate Chips
that's all there is to it
listen, honey, you got the talent
and nobody likes the fuller figure better'n me
but the Liz Taylor physique just ain't in
sure, I'll help ya, casting's in three weeks
so you'll eat celery and drink diet soda
till ya fit into a size ten cocktail dress
you'll look a million dollars
now go empty out your kitchen
and no cheatin cuz I'll be over
to check up on ya

15

The special today, ladies, is pastrami on rye
with side salad, choice of french fries or potato chips
and apple pie a la mode –
I'll be back in a minute, sweetie, to take your order.

Sure the kid's only 16 – but these days everybody
over the age of 8 knows the score.
My god, another day like yesterday and I'm
hanging up my track shoes and hair net.
We ran out of catsup in the middle of lunch
and some big-shot got a cockroach in his salad.

Did you watch the Miss America contest last night?
I was sure Miss Wyoming'd win. Then they announce
it's Miss Alabama and I nearly dropped my dentures.
It was a fix. Hey Joe, did that catsup ever get here?
You been to the sale at Wards yet? I've got to run over
on my break and look for a purse that'd
go with my new dress. It's our 30th anniversary
and the kids are giving us a surprise party.
The hairdresser was booked solid for a week,
so my sister's coming over later. She trained as a beautician.
Did you see the new kid they hired? Dracula's twin,
with fangs hanging down over her bottom lip.
Joe – while you're at it you might as well
get in more A-1 Sauce too.

You girls wanna order now?

16

well prepared
for the tropical heat and flies
of a high school lunchroom
I waded through a swamp of orange peels
hamburger buns candy wrappers and ballpoint pens
with a sun of endless fluorescent lights
beating on my brow
a flock of bananas floated majestically by
the natives could be seen squirting ketchup at each other
licking their fingers chewing and belching
some sat in a trance
rhythmically beating their plates with knives and forks
suddenly a brightly plumed aluminum toucan
appeared out of nowhere
soaring above our heads
the scene was disrupted
by a kind of gong in the distance
whereupon everyone stood up and left
but I was not discouraged
I was determined to stay
until I had at least sighted
a wild hot dog with its young
or heard the haunting call of the chocolate mousse
the enchanting grunt of the pig-in-a-blanket

17

oh yeah, it's an all-you-can-eat
salad buffet all right
but did you notice that your rear-end
barely fits on these chairs
and to get past the other tables
you have to hold your breath?
not only that, but every time you get up
with your plate you're surrounded by mirrors
telling you that your spare tyre
and midriff bulge are thriving
and that everyone in the place
is watching your blubber ripple
to top it all off the waitresses are thin as sticks
oh yeah, all-you-can-eat my eye

18

life holds no more unpredictable delights for me
I know now that if he asks me out
on Friday night it means a meal at Gino's
nothing personal against Gino
but it isn't exactly romantic to line up outside
for half an hour with every sort of rowdy
and once inside have to scream at each other
while we pull apart our triangles of pizza
and slurp beer from mugs
not that we never scream at each other
he always carves our initials in a heart
on the woodwork at our table
just so I won't get angry
when we have to go and park
down at the beach afterwards
so he can smooch
there are no surprises for me
if he calls on a Saturday
it means a movie and a chocolate shake

19

We press the button for 25
and look at ourselves going up in mirrors;
the crystals jiggle on the chandelier –
we pretend we don't notice.

On the 25th the fountain is gracefully spraying,
the magazine shop sells wooden dolls
as big as a child and as expensive.
We are seated at a round table with white
linen cloth, silver forks, statuesque goblets
next to an invisible card printed on
parchment that says, in wedding invitation letters
Do Not Be Vulgar. We try hard to obey:
napkins on our laps, voices turned down,
we order a little dish of dessert and coffee.
Our waitress sees through us –
we are not on our way to the airport, flying to Greece.
My mother and I go to restaurants,
imagining what it would be like
if we belonged in them.

20

the all-night supermarket
stood rubbing its eyes
trying to stay awake
boys mopped and yawned
labelled and stretched
unpacked and snored
the girl at the check-out
dreamed and turned over
opened the cash drawer for a cover
the cigarette display was her pillow
she talked in her sleep
about special offers
and have you entered our new competition
she watched sleepwalkers
leaving through automatic doors
lit by insomniac lights
carrying bags of moon dust
hibernating fish drooled
in their sea of ice
an ear of corn ground its teeth
and the potato's eye
danced under its lid
a lullaby on the muzak tape
brought even the coffee to slumberland

22

the film about some war
has just begun with a lion yawning
it is midnight
you make the refrigerator copy the lion
and our eyes starved for light
move across the terrain
hunting for the thing
our stomachs have always wanted
but never found
the light bulb on the side
shines through wire shelves
and makes the ceiling our cage
between sandwiches and tacos
the drama unfolds
some guy gets a bullet someplace
we find where the cookies were hidden
through the dark we hear bare feet
shuffling on bare floorboards
and hide the cookies
why aren't you kids in bed

23

it was hot and horrid
when we arrived
each of us carried something
through the park
to the picnic benches
we sprayed each other with insect repellent
and then sat watching aunts, uncles and cousins
clutching beach balls, barbecues and coolers
come across the baseball field towards us
more picnic tables were pulled over
and mountains of beef and potato salad
sandwiches, cookies, pretzels and cakes
were spread and everyone stuffed hands,
mouths and stomachs for a few hours
when the sun was low
their bodies resembled great walruses
resting on comfortable rocks

24

The first thing you say is
'May I help you Ma'am?'
If she answers 'I'm still deciding',
well then you reply
'Our choc-o-licious offer for today
is imported chocolate-covered cherries,
one dollar and ten cents a pound.
Would you care for a sample?'
She'll always say yes to that,
even if she knows all she wants
is a pound and a half of chocolate raisins.

Don't watch them while they're sampling,
except out of the corner of your eye:
it makes them self-conscious.
'My that *was* tasty,' she'll sigh,
as she wipes the syrup off her chin.
'How much did you say those were?'
'One dollar and ten cents, Ma'am,
will I give you a pound or two?'
'Well, I *am* trying to watch my waistline,
but I'll take a pound and a half
of chocolate raisins.'

Then you say 'Why Ma'am, you certainly
don't look like you need to count your calories.'
As you're shovelling the raisins onto the scale,
make sure she's watching and put a little extra in;
that way, when you say 'Will that be all?'
she may just giggle 'Oh I'm in a naughty mood today,
you can give me a pound of those cherries as well.'
Say 'Yes Ma'am' humbly, so she
won't notice you persuaded her.

25

around the dinner table
each of us leans over a white circle
picking up the flesh of animals
with metal implements
father is at the head of the polished wood

mother at the other end near the kitchen
no flies interrupt us – it is winter
tonight relatives have come to dine

this is lovely
pass the dinner rolls
take your elbow off the table
I must get your recipe
may I have more sauce
would you care for a second helping

a voice from the other
side of the foliage calls:
why don't you ever tell
your brother that you love him
it sounds like my brother's wife

from both poles of the table
I receive radio signals:
watch it they say don't get her started on *that* again
we clear our throats fiddle with napkins
wait anxiously for ice cream to slur our words
I concentrate on my white circle
where the bone of a chicken drowns
in a puddle of salad dressing

Dancer

I am a Degas dancer,
pausing before my performance
to fix my blue sash
and think about dancing.

My shoe fits well,
I'm glad I'm here,
though sometimes I ache
and have to rest.

You won't be able
to see the ballet.
So judge me on how I stand
near the barre or tie my shoe.

If I do them well
then I am just as great
as the greatest
of all dancers.

Three Paintings by Edward Hopper

I *Chop Suey*

'Isn't it fun to come down here
away from the kids
and eat in Chinatown
on a crisp afternoon?
After playing with our chopsticks
and drinking tea from those funny little cups,
we'll take the bus
to Saks Fifth Avenue or Bergdorff Goodmans
and try on expensive clothes.'

'Look out the window
at the restaurant sign –
all you can see is "Suey"
the "Chop" must be farther up.'

II *Nighthawks*

The heat and the dark
drive us from apartments
down empty streets
to the all-night diner
where fluorescent bulbs
illuminate us like tropical fish
in a fish tank.
We sit side by side
listening to glasses clank,
the waiter whistling,
and stare at air.
Not looking at our watches
or counting the cigarettes
and cups of coffee.

III *Automat*

I thought when I came here
I'd get rich as a secretary
and marry my boss.
I dreamt about that so long
I thought it would happen.
Maybe I should go back.

I hate small places though
and when I sit eating at the automat
I pretend I'm a celebrity
and all those walls of plastic doors
are really crowds of camera lenses
waiting to take my picture.

Bookworm

Opening a cabinet
under the kitchen sink,
I'm surprised to find
you leaning against a water pipe
reading *Myth and Ted Hughes.*

I'm drying the dishes now
and look out the window
to see you raking mud
with the *T.L.S.* on the handle
reading 'The Laureate of Ambiguity'.

How can you concentrate, I wonder,
carpet-sweeping a woven rug,
polishing a door knob,
with a book in your other hand
reading 'Language, you terrible surrounder...'

Even when you're sleeping
your dreams are literary:
walking up a steep dark staircase,
books, like bats, were flying at your head.
Reading the titles out loud saved you.

As I point the car towards work
you sit beside me with *American Poetry Review.*
Everyone is tired, waiting in a traffic jam;
I brake and honk and swear,
but you are reading 'Words are everywhere.'

The Object

Hold me only when necessary.
Put me back newly dusted off
and in the proper place.
Look at me from the correct distance
at the few moments every day
when the sun filters through the room
striking me at an advantageous angle.

Please try not to upset
my delicate composition.
Don't be tempted to change my position,
or demand more
than that I am here,
in the right lighting,
looking as best I can.

Bag

I have here
a plastic bag with handles

inside I carry a few pieces of myself
a spare arm, replacement vein, extra skin

they do come in useful
on days like today

Tea Break

The Queen deserves to be rich,
she works harder than us.
I was never as bored as by Chekhov.
You don't like anything.
I think capital punishment should be brought back.
What are you doing this weekend.
Did you watch that show on TV last night.
I'm reading *The Carpetbaggers*,
it's filthy but very good.
Don't they make a lovely couple.
I'm buying shoes at lunchtime.
The girl making tea has a tattoo on her arm.
How much would you say she earns.
I'm so fed up.
My driving lesson's on Saturday.
Who's doing the collection.
Do you like that new song.
We have the best education system in the world.
I'd never leave Ireland.
I saw this gorgeous dress.
My mother always says.
I've got a headache.
She makes me so angry.
How do you know.
That's just your opinion.

Chit-Chat

'The children?'
She thinks for a moment
between her fake eyelashes.
'They're fine.
The oldest girl is hiking
around Europe with her boyfriend
collecting peasant folk songs.
My first son has left us temporarily
for a religious cult out west.
They worship the sun
and aren't allowed to get married.
But I know my Arnie.
He'll be back here one of these days
listening to his stereo
and chasing after girls in no time.
Then there's my other daughter.
She's got a Japanese boyfriend.
She wears unusual clothes and says
they both want to be artists.
If you're ever passing through town
you might see their work.
They paint brick walls and fire hydrants.
The baby of the family
lives in an inflatable solar-powered house
with no water. He goes to a stream
several times a day with a pail.
He's very hearty and rustic.
I stayed with him once for a week
and even got used to the outhouse.
What are yours up to?'

Marketing

'Tell me honestly, now,
cause it's your age-bracket
we're targeting:
What do ya think?
It's a bucket, a plastic bucket.
You could put a plant in it,
fill it with water
and buy a goldfish,
bring it to the store
and put your groceries in it.
If you're into cleanliness
you could use it to mop the floor,
you can turn it upside down
and sit on it or use it as a table.
See, it's a product for
the alternative generation.
We're getting them printed up
with *The Fuck-it Bucket* in bright letters.
You'll have the choice of
a marijuana plant,
horoscope calendar, the peace sign
or a rainbow underneath the letters.
It's a symbol – it says:
"We've had it with your bourgeois containers,
this is what we're for:
a working-class bucket".'

He straightened his designer tie,
took a sip from his martini
and gazed down at the street 28 stories below.
'It'll be bigger than the hula-hoop.'

Chicawgo

In Chicawgo da truck drivers
an da newspaypa boys drive
der trucks and bikes aroun early in da A.M.
Da doughnut shop has two coppers

sittin in it every mornin;
der squads parked next ta each udder.
Day like der doughnuts covered
in chocolatey mush, but day don't like

da new Dago or A-rab or whatever da H he is
makin da coffee. It's lousy
when da law can't even get a decent breakfast.
Den around 8 all da robots go ta work.

My mudder hollers at me an I pretend
I'm asleep. Den dee ole man
turns on the WCFL traffic report full blast
right in my ear an I grunt

an tell him ta cut it out. Me an my buddies
have an ok time down at da garage.
We ain't soft in da middle like some people
I don't care ta mention.

Da Boss

(in memory of Mayor Richard J. Daley)

Dat guy knew how ta do tings:
He'd get ya a job or fill up da holes in da street
or just wave at ya from a parade
goin down State Street an ya could tell
he really cared about all a us.
I can't hardly believe he ain't aroun no more.
We used ta see him on da 6 o'clock news
while we was eatin our dinner
an no matter how tired we was
or how rotten the meatloaf
we'd always cheer up when we seen him
plantin a tree or smashin champagne on somethin
or tellin some chump of an alderman at City Hall
ta shut up an sit down.

Local Man Tells of Native City

Well, it's my kinda town for one.
Ya got yer Cubs, White Sox, Bears and Black Hawks
and as for that faggoty game they play
over there in Europe
– kick the ball – well I tell ya,
we got that one too
only I ain't gonna brag about it, see?
As for yer public recreation and leisure areas,
there's Lincoln Park which includes the Farm in the Zoo,
for the city kids to see cows and pigs
and whatnot such as just-born livestock
and it's always a big hit, stuff like that,
with my kids anyhow. Some a the company
in them places ain't too choice
as every pervert and louse seems to be
hanging around the park lately,
but for a Sunday outing yer safe enough.
Anywho, in a place like this, ya can't
exactly keep yer offspring in the dark
about weirdos and life in general
if ya know what I mean
with scumbags doin indecent things on the subway, etc.
Chicago's Finest ain't got the easiest job
in the whole wide world, and I always
make it easier for the boys
by keeping some dollars in my pocket
not to mention my twelve year old, Judy,
who's a genius at turning on
the water works in an emergency.
Then we come to State Street, that great street
where they do things they don't do on Broadway.
If ya want my advice you'll stick
to the east side a that place because
for I-don't-know-how-long the west side
is kinda seamy with discount emporiums.
If yer hungry go eat a sandwich or a piece of cake
in this joint called The Palmer House
and you'll feel like a hotshot in their cafeteria.
Wabash Avenue is my idea of a real man's street

with a capital M. It's murky and atmospheric cuz
the elevated tracks run overhead and it's lined with
camera stores, electrical stores and steak restaurants.
When you're driving down Wabash it's a challenge
avoiding the steel girders that hold up the tracks.
Abe Lincoln woulda liked Wabash Avenue I bet.
My sainted wife tells me that all the classy types
have moved up to North Michigan Avenue,
but from what I've seen it looks like a crowd
of conventioneers and suburbanites from hicksville places
like Cairo, Illinois and Dubuque, Iowa sporting laminated
name tags with *Hi, I'm Dorene* on them.
Ralph Lauren is up there, I admit,
but if my wife says the classy types hang out there,
well ya can bet yer bottom dollar they've cleared out
and left it for the Japs, hillbillies and bargain-hunters.
If you're really bored in summer, you can
observe the blub along the Lakeshore
or go out to O'Hare Airport and watch
everybody leaving and arriving or check
the phones for change – I once collected eight dollars.
Each time I roam Chicago keeps calling me home.
It's one town that won't let you down.

What's What

(1991)

In *Betty's of Winnetka*

Judy the sales assistant
is being praised at the moment
by Mrs Chester Finnerman:
'This little lady,' she announces to us,
'knows what's what about clothes.'
She gives Judy a gentle shove
on her left shoulder.
'She has helped me develop
my *entire* wardrobe.
She tells ya if yer tushy is too enormous
for a pair of pants
like it was outta the mouths of babes.
You guys know how it is
with people saying that kinda stuff –
but not with her. Oh no, she makes it sound
like it was a compliment!'
We stand at the pay desk in awe.
'She and she alone has stopped me
looking like a schmuck like I used ta.'
All of our eyes travel up and down Mrs Finnerman's edifice.
'Chester says it isn't right
that a woman of my years
should look so desirable.'

Adios

You shoulda seen
what a lump on a log I was.
I was the certified chauffeur
for all the family.
Dolly has piano lessons?
Dad'll drive you.
My wife is goin' to the Jewel Food Store?
Get old drippo to sit behind the wheel.
But it was more than that.
There were these eight people
all grabbing my dough
on a Friday night;
eight mouths waiting for Hamburger Helper,
and after I'd bought them
their Dream Whip and their Keds gym shoes
they start calling me a square.
I was corny they said.
My daughter called me a male chauvinist pig
cuz I was enjoying the half-time entertainment
with the Dallas Cowboys' cheerleaders
kicking up their heels.
This is a gyp, I told myself.
I can't even relax
during a crummy football game.
I got my car keys
and headed for sunny Florida.
So long chumps.

Content and Tasteful

Here I am in my kitchen.
I look content and tasteful.
When my darling grandchildren
visit their grandma, I give them
windmill cookies – the ones with chunks
of nuts that come wrapped
in the orange cellophane package
with scenes of old Holland.
In this oven I cook up a storm.
Ya gotta garnish your recipes.
Cut out pictures from magazines
like *McCall's* or *Family Circle*
and always make your dishes
look like in the photographs.
I keep a few tricks up my sleeve
in these cabinets only I don't tell them
to anybody except my daughter
in Sarasota Florida who's trying
to get to a man's heart
through his stomach.
That's the only exception.
Do you catch the aroma of my
Devil's Food Cake baking?
Ladies, don't waste your time
with most of these new appliances.
Get your basics, keep 'em clean, buy fresh,
and I guarantee you your mouth
will be watering and your girdle
will be killing you.

Well-heeled

So what's to live for?
I'm placing an American Express Gold Card
on the cash desk – seven hundred and fifty dollars
down the drain
for a fantasy rhinestone pump
with spike heels.
Yesterday, it was paisley-gilded
black brocade lace-ups with a louis heel.
My analyst said, 'Indulge.'
So I'm indulging already!
I think I'd rather have an affair.
My Grecian slave sandals
would come in handy for that
or maybe my fuchsia satin court shoes –
depending on the man.

I started my girls off right.
As soon as they put a foot on terra firma
I got them little Edwardian slippers:
pink sides with a white toe and bow.
I can still see them teetering along
with frilly cotton socks and Easter bonnets.
I have those shoes up in the attic someplace.
I wonder which box they're in…

Nobody gives a damn about shoes any more.
Will Sammy the Hong Kong mailman
want to seduce me in my red-rabbit-fur bedroom slippers?
Who's to appreciate – Glen, my spouse?
What a joke!
He trots off in his Gucci loafers to work
and you might as well be wearing
hiking boots under your negligee
for all he cares.
So I head for Neiman-Marcus Shoe Salon –
'the place for women who love shoes'.
If he doesn't notice my fantasy pumps
maybe he'll notice the bill next month
from American Express.

I owned a pair of Maud Frizon shoes once
that had cute fake watches on the ankle straps.
He kept mocking them by kneeling down in front of me
'to see what time it is'.

Did you tell that shrink of yours
about the Calvin Klein princess pumps
ya bought a year ago
and have never worn cause you say
they're too pretty to wear
or those Texan snake and pony skin
hand-tooled leather cowboy boots
that you wear to the supermarket –
did ya tell him that –
what does all this mean?
Glen always toys with the dramatic
rather than the mundane in our relationship.

It was a pair of white patent Mary Janes
that made me the way I am today.
I refused to unfasten the strap
out of its golden buckle.
I wore them to bed, to school,
to play in – I even took a bath
with them on once – they made me happy.
One morning I woke up
and they were gone.
Words cannot convey that catastrophe.

Last week I wore a sea-green
suede-fronded ankle-boot
on my head to a party.
I went barefoot.
Maybe this is a development.

Big Herms

Mothers of the world
I hope you aren't
in Big Herms Hot Dog Stand
for Mother's Day
like I am.
My girlfriends are out
having lunch
with their happy families
at the Ramada Inn smorgasbord.
'What the heck is this?'
I ask myself.
I look around at the clientele:
thugs, Hell's Angels, creepos.
Herm gave me a doggy-bag
with the remains
of my Mother's Day Special.
I drove out to a neighbourhood
where I'm anonymous,
ate my dog and slaw.
My kids live out on the coast.
Their mother and her humiliation
might as well be mustard
at the bottom of the bag.

Change

Are you a woman
between the ages of 49 and 51?
I bet you feel like
elbowing the person
beside you at the cucumber display
or making mean faces
at somebody
you don't even know
on your way to work
each morning.
Do you murmur nasty things
about the couple across the street
and want to belt those kids
making so much noise?
I can sympathise.
Only ladies, stop it.
That's a bad way to act.
Get a grip on your bio-rhythms.
Hormone Replacement Therapy
can have dramatic results.
Why not ask your doctor about it today?

Year-at-a-Glance

All you go-getters out there
who publish *Fire Safety Monthly*
and *Metal Trade Weekly*
or *Soap, Perfume and Cosmetics International*
or *Chemical Compounds*
quit putting those
ugly old year-at-a-glance
wall calendars in your magazines
every December
as if you're doing us
this enormous favour.
Why not have a pow-wow next time
and opt for a sun visor with logo
or a washable pocket pen organiser?
Something handy
and covetable
instead of graphically illustrating
a year full of empty boxes.

Germs on the Phone

You wouldn't believe
how many germs
you clowns have.
You are crawling
with lethal micro-organisms.
How can a guy
protect himself
from these mutant viruses
I frequently ask myself.
That's why I carry
a supply of plastic bags
with me at all times.
If I *must* use
a public telephone booth
I wrap the receiver
in a bag
before holding it to my head.
I run to the nearest garbage can
when I'm done
and dispose of all
your filthy cooties.

Wind

Who cares if I'm sitting
in this darn old consultant's office
propped up at my LCD screen
and my ultra-modern receptionist desk like a loser
with pots of Estée Lauder creams,
colours and fragrances invested on my being
so that some dope of a manager
can fling himself at me
because he's a mega-client?
'Take a mother's advice,' she kept saying,
'finish your college education
before Mr Right comes along,
or you'll regret it the rest of your life.'
I got a dumb B.A., a 'position of responsibility
in a high-powered, non-stop environment',
I got a bachelorette apartment
in a trendy neighbourhood, I got myself
a Bloomingdales credit card
and a sports car and so what?
Here I am filing my nails
looking out across Lake Michigan
scattered with teensy sailboats
being blown over by the wind.

Yuppie Considering Life in Her Loft Apartment

Jeff is such a bastard.
Like I can't handle it.
All I did was throw the silver fork
he'd left stuck for a week
in the mud at the base
of my weeping willow tree
in the general direction of his chest
and while it was en route added,
'What am I, your maid, lunkhead?'
He, as usual, moved *before* the fork
crash landed on his bicep and said,
'No prob, no prob', and those were
his last words to me on his way
out of my orbit and into the
gravitational pull of some dim bimbo.
Advice has been pouring in:
'One look and I told you –
he's a no-goodnik, but you said you
liked his shoes, so there's no point
talking to you is there?'
And, 'Cancel him off your hard drive,
revise your memory bank
and write a new programme –
who needs the louse anyway?'
And, 'Join the club. Ya wanna
come with me for a facial? –
Elizabeth Arden have a special offer.'
The part that really gets to me
is that I forgot everything I learned
in that Psychology course I took last year:
'The Male Ego and How to Cope With It'.

from OPENING LINES: DRAMATICULES

Auschwitz

I says to him, 'Cutie-pie, come out of that.'
I says, 'You're asking for it, Brad.
These people don't give a damn
if you saved-up for three years
to travel over here – they wouldn't care
if it was ten years and they seem
awful nasty – so I think you'd better
get the hell outta there real soon.'
He kept saying, 'Check the focus.
Have you included the whole scene?
Is there enough light? Check it again.
I can't afford another trip if you don't do it right.
Can you see my face?'
I took a few snapshots and said,
'You're gonna be murdered if you don't get out
of that rotten old gas oven.'

Bed and Breakfast

Um, excuse me and everything
but did you two sleep OK last night?
Ya see neither of us got a wink.
That lady said the bed we'd have
was like a Queen-size and what it really was
was a three-quarter, right Fred?
Fred and me are used to a Queen-size.
We've had one since our honeymoon.
Maybe here in Ireland a three-quarter is a Queen-size –
but not in the States, I-can-tell-you!
Gee, we could hardly breathe.
You've gotta really cute country
only Fred and I'd be better off at home
if a three-quarter is a Queen-size.
We'd be too tired to see it.

Matinee

Grandma, whisper, everybody's turning around.
– Well is she being thrown out of the convent?
No, she's just going to be a governess for a while.
– What does she have on?
A brown dress, hat and she's carrying a suitcase.
– Where's she headed, is she walking or what?
Yeah, she's walking to the house where she got the job.
– Why didn't they pick her up in a carriage?
So she could sing a song on the way.
– Is this a true story?
I guess so.
– Well I bet they picked her up.
Now she's meeting the family.
– She marries the father, Ingrid told me.
He's very handsome and rich.
– I thought you said she was still a nun.

The Ballgame

Mel
– Yeah
Quit watching that baseball game
– Pipe down and get me a Bud
Mel
– Whadya want
Let's go see a movie er something
– Nah, this next guy might hit a grand slam
Mel
– Go with Shirley er Audrey
I wanna go with my husband
– My god, right the hell outta the ball park
Mel
– Knock it off
I wish WGN would go out of business
– Fat chance blabber mouth

Off the Rails

It was kinda scary how he was just staring
like a lunatic at the ingredients
on the cornflake box. I kept an eye on him
pretending not to and said, 'Stanley, what's a matter
with you anyhow? Why don't ya eat-up
or you'll miss yer train?'
He just said, 'shut-up' and it wasn't
really like him to say that to me.
'That's a great thing to say to me,
when it's 8.23 and the train goes
at 8.30 exactly and ya still haven't
eaten breakfast.' He just picked up his spoon
and commenced tapping his cereal bowl
real slow like a bell.
He stayed up in his room until midnight.
That was just the start of the problem.

Brats

Tell Wanda ta shut her trap, Mom.
– What's wrong with humming, knucklebrain?
Mom, will ya tell her?
– I can hum when I want – right, Mom?
Not while I'm watching something, sap.
– Reruns of the *Beverly Hillbillies*?
Mom, tell her or I'll bash her one.
– Your son is threatening me, Mother.
Wait till Dad gets home, smarty pants.
– Oh, I'm *so* scared!
Why don't ya tell her to shut her big dumb mouth?
– Quit bossing Mom around.
No, stupid, put a cork in it.
– He called me stupid, Mom.
I'm watching something you goddamn moose.
– Now, Mom, he's swearing.

Mom and Dad's Bedroom

It has a lived-in look.
A coffee mug is covered
with a Commonwealth Edison bill
which itself is partly obscured
by a pearl necklace and *Health* magazine.
No perfectionist sleeps here –
a shirt balances on its head
in the corner beside tights
that have gone flabby on the floor.
Keys hang from a pegboard.
A note speared to the door with a fork reminds:
'fill in every check stub.'
Every millimetre of living-space is filled in;
an oriental carpet is decorated with
a cake plate, a letter from California,
an Aran sweater, a psychedelic kite,
a popped button, an umbrella hat,
an L.L.Bean catalogue, a vitamin catalogue,
a bicycle brochure and a *New York Times*
Travel Section turned to 'What's doing in Antwerp'.
My Mom and Dad are watching TV
over the tops of their toes.
Three aerials scour the void
for signals from downtown Chicago.
Instead of a dial to change channels,
an enormous spoon protrudes from the control panel
with a big tie-up boot balanced by its shoelaces
on the handle
for a more realistic picture.

What We Talk About

About so and so and whatchacallit
being such louses
or else about what the hell
does this pea brain think he's doing.
Sometimes we discuss topics
to discuss on a BIG DATE,
but first we chew over the gear
the hair the accessories the war paint.
Don't say chew or we'll blab
about craving pineapple upside down cake
and the pig-out last week at Jennifer's.
When someone comes into the office
we've got the ugly skirt cheap blouse
clashing sweater bad skin
corny hair-do and she's awful fond of herself
to mull over for a while.
Then it's back to how crummy the weather is
should we book a sun-bed
the clothes dilemma: to put a deposit
or not to put a deposit
the length of the day
the temperature of the room
the cost of hand cream.
The boss says quit talking –
which should come in handy
as the main topic at break-time.

Managing the Common Herd

two approaches for senior management

THEORY X: People are naturally lazy.
They come late, leave early, feign illness.
When they sit at their desks
it's ten to one they're yakking to colleagues
on the subject of who qualifies as a gorgeous hunk.
They're coating their lips and nails with slop,
a magazine open to 'What your nails say about you'
or 'Ten exercises to keep your bottom in top form'
under this year's annual report.
These people need punishment;
they require stern warnings
and threats – don't be a coward,
don't be intimidated by a batting eyelash.
Stand firm: a few tears, a Mars Bar,
several glasses of cider with her pals tonight
and you'll be just the same old
rat-bag, mealy-mouthed, small-minded tyrant
you were before you docked her
fifteen minutes pay for insubordination.

Never let these con-artists get the better of you.

THEORY Z: Staff need encouragement.
Give them a little responsibility
and watch their eager faces lighting up.
Let them know their input is important.
Be democratic – allow all of them
their two cents worth of gripes.
(Don't forget this is the Dr Spock generation.)
If eight out of twelve of them
prefer green garbage cans to black ones
under their desks, be generous –
the dividends in productivity
will be reaped with compound interest.
Offer incentives, show them
it's to their *own* advantage to meet targets.
Don't talk down to your employees.

Make staff believe that they
have valid and innovative ideas
and that not only are you interested,
but that you will act upon them.

Remember, they're human too.

The Season To Be Jolly

I *A Blizzard on Judson Avenue*

A family in Eskimo coats waddles past on snowshoes
and a black poodle wearing a tartan ensemble
tiptoes by with red boots.
Two girls in striped hats
struggle through the powdery drifts
with their tongues out, trying to catch a snowflake.
A young executive, with a Christmas tree trunk
at his neck, groans and leaves a mark
like the dragging tail of a peacock.
I open the crystal window and listen for life.
There is no sound anywhere
except the scraping of a sled
piled with grocery bags
gliding down the middle of the street.
By morning, wind and snow
will have repaired the damage.

II *Woman Going to Christmas Party*

Now that the babysitter's here,
and the kids in their pjs
are hypnotised by Snoopy's Christmas Show,
I can take my hair-rollers out
and put some glitter on my eyelids.
Unfortunately, my youngest puked
on the shoulder of my party-dress,
so I've borrowed a sequinned shawl
from next-door and added extra perfume.
Beside the phone, I've left a list
of dos-and-don'ts and a number where,
if all else fails, I can be reached.
Chuck is outside warming up the engine;
but now for the fun part:
digging the car out of a snow-drift.

III *Santa*

Sometime around Thanksgiving
the missus goes all mush-mash on me
and I can tell stormy weather's ahead.
'Oh Herb-honey,' she says in her
I-just-spent-a-million-dollars-on-a-dress voice,
'the ladies of the Evanston Women's Club
have given you the supreme honour
of voting you this year's Santa Claus.'
I quit chewing a mouthful of apple pie,
drop (simultaneously) paper, fork, lower jaw
and reply, 'Huh?' as my left hand
clutches my forehead for effect.
So here I sit, with Lester Pugh casting a cynical eye
at my Mr-Nice-Guy act as he says,
'Mr Nelson, you ain't Santa Claus.
My mom said we could go and see Santa
and you're just the guy from across the street!'
'Ho, ho, ho, little boy,' I retort, 'Santa only brings
Star Wars spaceships to *good children.*'
'I'll be good, Santa,' says Lester, sprouting horns.

IV *Snow*

Don't get me wrong, I'm not a killjoy.
But did you ever spend four hours
using a shovel, a pick
and everything short of dynamite
to clear the sidewalk of ice and snow
so that little old ladies
could waddle to the store for parakeet seed
and so I. Magnin's and Bonwit Teller's Christmas catalogues
could be delivered to each consumer
and so the hoodlums wouldn't fall and fracture
their necks as they break into somebody's house;
and go to bed with a pain in yer back
like nobody's business
and blisters on yer hands
and wake up the next morning
to look out at three feet of snow on the sidewalk?

Dubuffet's *Winter Garden*

Bring a hat, mittens and scarf
if you plan to stay for more than five minutes.
Frostbite can be painful.
Anyone not wishing to visit winter
should proceed to the Impressionists:
if you can't stand the cold
get out of the igloo.
As you sit on a snow bank
gazing at the permafrost
listen carefully and you will hear
the wind plotting a blizzard.
You will notice the tracks and footprints
of trappers and huskies, polar bears,
arctic wolves and snow leopards.
None of these will disturb your visit
to the winter garden – normally;
they're only allowed in after closing.
Let's step into the second chamber.
Your sandal has disappeared in the snow?
Your mini-skirt is frozen solid?
Your walrus moustache is dripping icicles?
What do you expect when you come dressed for Tahiti?
Your nose is red, your teeth are chattering,
I suggest you join your friends
in front of that Gauguin.

In the Garden of Earthly Delights

(for John and Nuala)

I lean back into a flowery cushion
to see a rosebud creeping skyward behind my head.
The breeze, a wafting violin,
serenades your dancing sun-umbrella.
A sparrow tweets so much
it has to wet its whistle
at the stone bird-bath.
A crunchy strawberry thing melts on my tongue,
globs of cream beckon.
A carefree day sipping wine,
a row of geraniums on the windowsill humming.
A shy mezzo-soprano opens a window –
or is she singing through the crack
where the french doors are twinkling?
She looks around, anyway,
from her hide-out and decides on Mahler.
How did you train the bees on your foliage
to do those dexterous little tricks?
I want to put all this stuff
into a bottle and display it like a ship.

Bye

This is today –
the day I will wave at you
from a bus
a departure lounge
a moving car
a doorway.
It is more civilised
than sobbing
or hysterics –
no gnarly scenes
of naked sorrow
are called for.
Put your hand up:
decide if you want
finger twiddles
or arm activity.
Either way
keep up the momentum.
Don't remember anything
you meant to say or do.
Keep distance your goal.
All of us can create
wonderful excuses
for staying
where we are.
That's why we invented
the hand-flap
and the easy-to-lip-read
'Bye'.

Remind Me

I said – listen carefully –
you have crossed the Rocky Mountains
on a plane full of Indonesian immigrants.
You landed in Los Angeles
and saw tall palm trees
and then flew north to San Francisco
so don't play innocent.
You were met at the airport
and used the walk-o-lator to view
the exhibition of Mexican skeleton art.
I kept pleading with you to focus
what attention you could possibly muster
on the Chinese food in front of you.
The metaphorical drive over that
Golden Gate Bridge was beyond
your capacity to grasp.
You do recall the back and forth
hither and thither road to Bolinas
and how it was dark in the mountains – don't you?
The car veered either right or left
onto a gravel lane and then
you stumbled up the porch steps.
Does any of this ring a bell?
There was a ladder with carpet-covered rungs
up to the sleeping area.
Say you remember that much!

We were driving to a new mall
in third gear in a Volkswagen camper –
and I kept telling my sister
to shift into fourth.
I stood staring at the latest technology
in toothbrushes, home alarms,
talking car accessories, personal organisers.
At another town a Danish butcher
told us how to successfully barbeque a salmon.
We chewed corn chips while travelling.
The Joy of Cooking *was propped open*
to page 621: Marble Angel Cake.

A red hummingbird in a hand.
I left the station wagon and threw up
facing a peeled trunk of eucalyptus.
Someone had dropped his trousers
outside the dry cleaners in Mill Valley.
Burn-outs lounged in the parks in Berkeley.
You could hear blow-outs
from the children of the burn-outs
through a clearing behind the bushes.
People were swimming in a volcanic lake.
Buddhist monks farmed under a cliff.
What was it again you loved
in the antique clothes shop in Olema?
I couldn't explain the outside world to you,
it was too far away
and didn't sell frozen yogurt.

I tried again to remind her – what about the man
at the foster home – didn't he ask you
how to spell Bhopal
while he sat at his word-processor?
You must have gone out the kitchen door
at some stage to pick mulberries for a pie
because you had purple hands
and red scratches after that.
It smelled like a dream baking.
Does it seem any clearer?
What you need to find
is the silky tassle pull of that time.
Once you have it in your fist
you can recover it back from nowhere.
The kitchen was where you left from.
Trace over the road to Dogtown
past the church, the lagoon, the organic farmer.

It is on your planet –
you could get there right now if you tried.
The fake New England houses
built for nostalgic Californians
on Skywalker Ranch
are somebody's hang-up.
You could go out
and invent some hang-ups
of your own.

Dumbarton Oaks Library

I say good morning to the museum guard.
He slams the heavy door closed behind me
and announces that the magnolias are in bloom today.
I am in the glass-roofed passageway
but I call over my shoulder,
'Really? I must take a look at them.'
Beside me in a display case,
a pre-Columbian turquoise bead
is resting in two tiny brass hands.
Four marble steps lead into the breezy corridor.
I creak past the ballroom and drawing-room
with drapes flapping their arms at me.
Inside the stuffy wooden office upstairs,
I move a pile of catalogue cards,
rearrange stacks of books,
give the table a shove
and open the huge window.
Outside in the formal gardens,
two men are looking for a contact lens
lost in the flower beds.
I lean over the windowsill thinking
so that's a magnolia.

The Great Blasket Island

Six men born on this island
have come back after twenty-one years.
They climb up the overgrown roads
to their family houses
and come out shaking their heads.
The roofs have fallen in,
birds have nested in the rafters.
All the whitewashed rooms
all the nagging and praying
and scolding and giggling
and crying and gossiping
are scattered in the memories of these men.
One says, 'Ten of us, blown to the winds –
some in England, some in America, some in Dublin.
Our whole way of life – extinct.'
He blinks back the tears
and looks across the island
past the ruined houses, the cliffs
and out to the horizon.

Listen, mister, most of us cry sooner or later
over a Great Blasket Island of our own.

The Sounds of Earth
(broadcast from Voyager-II to the universe)

First, the most popular sound:
we call it talking – it is also known fondly as
shooting one's mouth off, discussing,
chewing the fat, yammering, blabbing,
conversing, confiding, debating, blabbing,
gossiping, hollering, and yakking.
So here's a whole bunch of jaw creakers.
How come none of you guys out there
don't yap at us – we'd sure like to hear
what you have to say
on the subject of where the hell you are.

For our second selection,
we will now play a medley of music
which you may or may not care for
since as I know myself
music is a very personal thing.
Why not aim a little musical extravaganza earthward?
As I say, we're waiting.

Now for our something-for-everyone finale.
Here's a rush hour traffic jam,
brakes are screeching – horns are blasting.
This is a phone ringing, a keyboard tapping,
and a printer whirring in the background.
I'm very partial to this next example of earth sounds:
a rocking chair creaking back and forth on a porch
accompanied by birds and crickets chirping.
To finish up, we've got a lawn mower,
knitting needles, a hammer, a saw,
a football stadium after a score,
a door shutting, a baby crying
and the ever-popular drone of television
blaring across the airways.

We're equal opportunity down here
so if you're a blob or have three heads
or look like something the cat dragged in –
we won't bat an eyelid.

Swivel Shelf

Not only is it impossible
to stay inside tonight
but it is equally impossible
to go anywhere.
That's when the cabinets
in the kitchen come into their own.
It is the open and close
look up look down
move the can of soup over to the left
and stack the box of lasagne
on top of the box of rice game.
You know how you hate
a pub's smoky atmosphere:
thank your fate
for producing cabinets
with swivel shelves
so you can enjoy taking stock
of the non-perishables
without that upsetting position
where you kneel down,
open the door
and insert your head fully.

Getting Through the Night

I

We part ways for the night.
I slip inside a dream bag
and zip it up when the last toe
is losing consciousness for another day.
If you didn't turn on the light at eight,
who knows how long I'd sleep?
Your nightime vistas are strewn
with hovering airplanes,
or poets soberly discussing
literary points in calf-bound rooms.
Sometimes I can hear you
pounding on the ceiling of my dreams
for me to turn the noise down.

II

I was upstairs in a loft
or on one of those sleeping devices
that are always being invented
on Judson Avenue.
Maybe I was copying out
a poem onto the wall
we use for poetic graffiti.
Maybe I was only reading
when I heard you calling
'Julie, Julie' from downstairs.
'WHAT?' I screamed
so loudly that I woke myself up
three thousand miles and fifteen years away.

III

I don't ask myself
what I'm doing snoozing in a bed
in a pitch black room
in a house enveloped
in misty fog on fields
located in the middle of nowheresville
somewhere on an island
out floating in tons of H_2O.

The end result might
overload my fuses.
I merely stick my nose
out from under the puffy quilt
and listen closely
to the intercontinental jet overhead
and imagine passengers
slumped in seats
mouths hanging open
trying to catch a few winks
before they encounter loved ones
on the far side of the planet.

Leaving Home

The first night
you'll lie face-down and cry.
That helps to clear your head.
In the morning, you aren't sure
what to do about breakfast
since you're in a strange house.
You unfold the map
your father gave you
and follow the mark
of his felt-tip pen
along the outlines of streets
that seemed impossible
to imagine last week
but now stalk right outside.

Saturday Afternoon in Dublin

Dietrich Fischer-Dieskau is in the process
of depressing me singing
the 'Der Einsame im Herbst' section
of *Das Lied von der Erde*.
A flute is playing as I look
at my sisters photographed in New York
in a crowd of twenty-five thousand people
getting ready for a bicycle tour.
I meet them for a few days
every two years or so
but I don't know them any more;
only how they used to be
before I went away.
Are you crying yet?
Sometimes you get to know your relatives
better when they're pinned down
like butterfly specimens
wearing baseball cap and crash helmet respectively.
Kate, I see, has a blue-faced watch
with snappy red band.
Ellen has let her hair grow.
They both smile nervously
because my father is taking the picture
in the middle of the throng.
Dietrich, meanwhile, has moved on to a beautiful, sad,
song with harps – I'm glad I don't know any German –
it's even sadder hearing words sung
that make no sense.
He says, 'Ja, ja' better than anyone.
It isn't music for New York, really.
A Hopper etching: 'Night Shadows',
an afternoon in Dublin looking
out the arid window for inspiration,
wanting so many things to happen –
that's when it gets to you.
Are you crying yet?

Moon Message

I was following the dancing ball
of the moon until it hopped
into a cloud and hid.
Someone in my vicinity
was smoking in the No-Smoking car.
I'm surrounded by Irish people
with a lady nagging at her kid,
'Patrick, come on, we're getting off the train.'
I can't blame the Irish
for travelling on a train
in their own country –
it just surprises me
to be in such a foreign location.
Me and my Maxwell House paper cup
seem to be the only Yankee products
roaming to Limerick
through the peat smoke and bushes.
I like to think of the moon as a Yank.
He saw me looking out a car window
in 1967 coasting down the outer-drive
beside Lake Michigan.
I whispered something to him.
Tonight, for the first time,
I can hear him answer back.

Café – Dempster Avenue

if you sit in the café
surrounded by
raw brick
raw wood
and folk music
the man
at the next table
will talk to you
and you
should talk back
don't just come
and read the paper
in the café
expecting coffee
and banana bread
that isn't
the point
at all

Misty Island

Sei Shonagon's *Pillow Book* tells
how the smell of pine torches
wafts through the air
and fills your carriage
when you're travelling through the dark
in a procession someplace.

Here on this island in the fog,
I'll have to take her word – 'delightful' – for it.
As I read the part where she says
'is wafted through the air and pervades
the carriage in which one is travelling',
'Down by the Salley Gardens' starts playing on the radio.

No Can Do

(2000)

Schmooze-Fest

They bought my life
so I'm off to Lake Geneva, Wisconsin
for a corporate bonding weekend.
I'll get through this schmooze-fest
if it's the last thing I do.
Marv says avoid the loser
in the snappy tie.
He says pack a jumbo bottle
of *Bug-Off* – those little varmints
can be murder.
There goes my watch alarm.
Time for a whacky round
of executive whirlyball.

Weather

What are ya – slow?
Don't you get it?
Once we sent up those darn astronauts
and all that space garbage
to the outer atmosphere
it wrecked the weather.
For crying out loud
you can't keep puncturing
the sky with those items.
Where do ya think
all the oxygen's going?
It's leaking out the holes, stupid.
Any dummy knows that.
You can hardly breathe any more.

Home

The Illinois sunrise demonstrates
exactly what an alien you are
in your car on the prairie
heading north to Chicago
where some Irish guy
aimed a hundred years ago.
That's why you're going there
instead of somewhere else.

He is controlling your life
and the direction of your auto.
If he had decided on Boston –
you'd be driving there instead.
Funny how we let this geezer
place us here and give us an accent,
expecting us to live surrounded
by corn and soybean fields.

In a booth at the Dixie Truck Stop
you drink your bottomless coffee
and figure how the rustics to your left
and the military personnel to the rear
were similarly plonked down
in the middle of nowhere.
Simple souls that we are
we now call this region 'Home'.

Bagels, Snow

I don't want to
do one of these
'sitting in a bookshop
during January
eating bagels
with my sister
whilst watching
the falling snow
in downtown Chicago
as the lights come on
at dusk' type of deals.
But she is drinking
an oversized cup of cocoa,
there are shelves of reassuring books
beside us, white lights decorate
the winter branches outside
and the tragedy hasn't happened yet
so I need to keep
the snow sparkling,
the cocoa steaming,
the bagels waiting
on a white plate
for as long as possible.

No Can Do

I know I'm a total party-pooper.
But there's no way
I can go to Red Lobster.
I have to stay home.
I have to rest.
I can't move.

Chip is like:
'How come you don't want to
to go out anyplace?'

I'm this huge moose
with no hair,
a cheapo wig and cancer.
And I'm supposed to go
and eat a Seafood Platter?
No can do.

Sipper Lids

It didn't feel so hot
when I found out about
those sipper lids.
We were driving to hardware stores
like it was the good old days.
The air was July
and the sun was too.
'Don't put the brownies
on the dashboard – they'll melt.'
I'm pulling off the lid
on my honey-sweetened coffee,
when my dad tells me not to.
'Watch me' – he picks up his coffee,
puts the lid to his mouth.
(He's doing this and steering.)
As I look over at him
sipping from the little gashes
in the plastic lid,
I know all is lost.
I might as well have been
the older kid from Italy
stuck at the back
of our Chicago classroom
because she didn't speak English.
Some kind of foreigner
who never heard of sipper lids.

Hogging the Chow

I would love to know
who's hogging all the chow
down at that end.
It would interest me greatly.
Do I have to send a
SWAT team over there
to commandeer a few lumps of squash
and a handful of peas?
I seem to recall shelling out
for all this stuff.
Is that the smell of fried chicken in the air
or am I hallucinating
due to lack of nutrition?
My sainted wife
has been turned into stone
with her mouth hanging open
and a bowl of mashed potatoes
hovering three inches off the table.
Let's try banging our plates
with our cutlery.
It works in prison movies.

McDougalmeister's

OK. Time for a chow-down
at McDougalmeister's.
Order me a McChicken Grilled Sandwich,
a McEskimo Double Fudge Sundae,
a McDougalmeister Large Fries.
Oink Oink.
Your ketchup is dripping down
your Disney t-shirt, Mr Slobola.
Lick it off Mickey's ear – feel free.
Are you with me here, people?
This is the pace we're working for:
one-two-three-four-five.
Any dilly-dallys or dawdlers
will get forty lashes
with a wet noodle.
We've got three hundred cornfields
to get through
until we can fill our pie-holes again
at the next McDougalinsky's.

Skinny

All I ever eat is cake.
I eat it at every meal.
Oh and I drink Snapple.
First I take a forkful of cake,
then I wash it down with Mango Cocktail.
That's my secret
on how come
I'm so skinny.

Reflected

in the milky mirror of tea
is my face
looking at the painting
'Flatiron Building Reflected
in Car with Figure in Bus'.
I can almost see both reflections
at the same time.
That isn't all I can do.
I hear three or four things, too.
A magpie's click, an orchestra,
street drill and keyboard
as I hold the cup to my mouth
looking over the rim
at the Richard Estes painting
and read: 'probably the first picture
I did of reflections + cars'.
Add to that how, as I put down the mug,
I just thought I'd love to write some poems
that feel like these paintings.
Occasionally, everything seems clear,
reflected in everything else.
I won't tell how I had the tea mug
in one hand and a pen in the other,
watching, drinking and writing
at the same time –
you'd think I was showing off.

Not a Nice Place

Holy cow!
You should see that place.
Children have bulletproof backpacks
for their schoolbooks.
People are four feet around.
Men wear skirts,
women power-dress.
All they ever do is complain
about their charcoal-grilled steaks.
It is not a nice place.
War surgeons train in city hospitals
– oi vei, you could get shot
for your Rolex watch
or your Nike boots
or if you look crooked at somebody
on an interstate highway.
Everybody there is weird.
Killer bees go on the rampage.
Lost children are advertised
on milk cartons.
People say 'Have a nice day' to you.
Nuts hide in the woods
with Uzi sub-machine guns.
A grassy hill might be a nuclear silo.
Garbage is pulverised
to the size of a shoe box.
How can people
live like that?

Short-changed

The gals behind the hosiery counter
have looks of despair on their faces.
Is this any way to leave a cash drawer,
with no quarters or dimes or singles?
How the heck are they supposed to sell
pantyhose without any change?
A customer unfurls a tale
of New Year's Eve hose-horror:
finding a hole near the butterfly
at her ankle when she put them on.
Her entire evening in shreds,
she wore a plain pair.
Hon, look at these snags –
you said you never wore them.
The verdict arrives:
See if there's another pair out.
(Wear them New Year's Eve,
bring them back and get a new pair –
why not?, they mutter.)
And just wait till they get their hands
on the girl who left them no change.

The Long Room Gallery

Trinity College Dublin

There is nothing to breathe
here in the Gallery
except old years.
The air from today
goes in one lung
and 1783 comes out the other.
As for spirits,
stand perfectly still
and you will feel them
carousing near your ear.
Tourists down below
think they've seen a ghost
when they spot you
floating through bookcases
over their heads.
On a creaky wooden balcony
you tunnel through centuries,
mountains of books
rising into the cumulus.
You could scale a ladder
up the rockface of knowledge
or search the little white slips
stuck in books
for a personal message
from Swift.
Ancient oxygen,
antique dust particles,
petrified wood...
Who are you kidding?
You belong down there:
baseball caps, chewing gum, videos.

Book Look

What look are you going for?

Let me guess.
I see books and an antique globe.
Am I getting warm?
Colours – OK – I'm seeing bright and dark,
I'm seeing wood and flowers,
I'm seeing hand-woven throws
and wrought-iron chandeliers
where you can attach real candles.
How am I doing?
Are we on the same planet here?
Now it's starting to gel.

I'm visualising a tribal rug,
a wall covered in frames.
Am I headed in the right direction?
So really, what we're talking about
is Ralph Lauren Country House.
You know where they're all in some
moth-eaten mansion in jolly old England
filled with conversation pieces
from like Rangoon or someplace?
Lots of books strewn around.
Books! Oh I just love that Look.

Three-week Residency
a found poem

Here is little me
coming to immerse myself
in poetry in a Zen-like room
with wall-length desk
and a window displaying
sub-tropical foliage:
a 'mid-career worker bee
buzzing around that fragrant creature,
our Master Artist'.

My Master instructed me
to write with long lines.
I am like the chameleon
outside my cell
which ope'd its ruby mouth.
I swallow Her advice.
Hark – I will grow
resplendent enough
for a glittering New York publisher.

The Master Artist invites us
to her cottage to discuss Heavy Metal.
She is no stranger to popular music
in general – she danced for 20 minutes
to a Grateful Dead tape.
Know what she is doing?
Pressing the sufficiency of the lyric.
She wants to follow the stutter-step
of tangential discussion.

Our writing grew luxuriant
and expansive, longer-lined.
Master Artist, you effected
a memorable encounter
with artistic Otherness:
you invited painters to a pot-luck supper.
They marched in with Caesar salad,
taco salad, spinach salad, casseroles,
home-made cookies – you name it.

Those painters! They joshed around,
laughed uproariously at unexpected moments,
razzed each other and did not act
like misanthropic Cézannes
or reclusive O'Keeffes at all.
We poets are teetotallers, wholegrainers –
hardly the Rimbaud set.
We slunk off apologetically to bed –
we are early risers.

'There is this matter of the shuttle launch'
our Master declared one evening.
We would congregate and walk
to a suitably pastoral space to view it.
We all felt the need to observe
such an assertion of earthly might
from the proper perspective.
Who would be the first to convert it
into a *New Yorker* acceptance?

On my last afternoon
I stopped by the Master's cottage.
Despite her tooth problem,
she was perky – I couldn't resist
relating a story about a manatee
I had patted on the head.
I also assured her that my lines now
terminated only when they encountered
the margins of my computer screen.

Trust my Master to see the connection
between the shuttle-launch
and patting the manatee!
A classic piece of metaphysical wit
which looks over its shoulder
at Disney World with visionary 'lift-off'.
Ho-hum, these darn old virtuosos
connecting themselves
to the mind-boggling experience
of being alive.

Writing

I got
real good
grades
in my
poetry workshop.
It was
tough though
revealing my
secret feelings
to a bunch
of people
I didn't know –
but it was
worth it
for a
good grade.

Old Babes

The old babes
feed the pigeons.
They got the circular
about pests on balconies
and chose to ignore it.
Who else is going to drop by
and be glad to see them?
Not their big-shot son.
Or their grandchildren
with buzz-cut hair-dos.
It's pigeons or nothing.

Oh Mom

I

Mom and I are out driving.
We drive up Irish mountains,
we drive down Irish boreens,
we peer over Irish cliffs.
It is almost time
for our coffee break
in a cozy craft emporium.
We could handle a fruit scone
just about now, too, right Mom?
Sometimes you have to stop looking
at those darn stone walls
and those blasted cute little kids
and drink something to remind you
of your home on Sheridan Road –
apartment 22C.

II *Bunratty Folk Park*

Mom and I are at the tourist attractions.
Even when it's raining
and our hair-dos
are one gigantic frizz-ball,
we don't wimp-out.
If the next exhibit
seems to be an authentic
fisherman's cottage (rocks hanging
on the thatch so the roof won't blow off)
we go with the flow
and take a few snapshots.
Say there are fifty 11 year-olds
eating their packed lunches
in the steamy tea-shop, does it bug us?
No way – it's a happening.
Outside, every shape puddle
you could ever dream of!

Hey Mom, it's time to go down
to the genuine old-time Irish village
so hold up that umbrella,
keep your camera handy
and prepare to stroll
right back into the past.

III *Jury's Cabaret*

We even almost get
a tear in our eye
when the guy in the leprechaun suit
sings 'Danny Boy'.

IV *Grub*

Mom and I would like to say
that the chow just wasn't *us*.
How many french fries
can one person eat
before their plumbing clogs?
But, we will admit
it was an interesting experience
and it reminded us of
those animal-fat-ridden
days of yore.

V *Blarney at Killarney*

I think I can speak for us both
when I say we wouldn't have minded
if somebody could've killed the rain.
It wouldn't have bothered us
in the least if the sun had come out.
So Mom and I decided
to take a tour boat – 'The Lily of Killarney' –
to shelter from the dampness.
No dice.
Too windy on the lakes.

We checked into a hotel
and looked down at tubercular horses
waiting to haul tourists through town.
We gave ourselves a pep-talk:
'This is ancient Irish rain –
the real McCoy – get into it!'
Then we found the tastiest
lobster soup in the North Atlantic
to heat our guts.
A luxurious bath, a little TV:
Mom and I were new gals.

Alla Luna
a lunar cycle

Last summer
we lived
on the planet
of purest sadness
looking at people
in the streets
like aliens –
looking at each day
as if it were the last.
We spoke to the moon
without words,
without hope.

          *

There was a blue pool
in the sky.
We liked swimming
up there when the moon
and some stars
floated in the water.
You had to be careful
not to butterfly
through a cloud
or dog paddle
into the universe.

          *

What was the deal last summer?
We were surrounded
by sky in all directions.
If it wasn't dawn over the lake
it was dusk over the buildings.

Not to mention lightning,
orbiting sky furniture
like stars, planets,
then examining the moon
through your telescope.
All we ever did
was try to sit still
holding our breath
watching the heavens
for a sign.

*

Oh really –
let's all gaze at the moon
and have a nervous breakdown
since life stinks.
I was looking at the lake sideways,
my head on a pillow
wishing and wishing
you would get better.
The moon went blurry:
space-garbage sneering
at me and my sadness.

*

A year ago
I stood at the window
high in the sky crying.
I focussed my father's telescope,
saw lunar mountains, craters, valleys.
'Well, moon,' I said,
'How can I ever be happy again
when my father is disappearing
to a place I can't visualise?'
Luna, I watched you change
all summer into a harvest moon
just before he died.

*

If you were still
in this solar system
we'd be e-mailing
comet sightings
to each other like crazy
and you'd have flipped
watching Hale-Bopp
through your skyscraper windows
on Sheridan Road.
But now I guess
you're some kind of asteroid yourself
travelling to wherever.
Great timing, Jack.
You're missing everything.

The Deal

It cost everything
but he bought a year.
And once it was his
he owned the sky,
a couple of volcanoes
and every molecule
in the universe.
He figured it was pricey
but hey – it was all his.
Minutes and quarter hours
were his as far
as the eye could see.
As for months, twelve big ones
all in a row.
By the time his
daily desk diary
was down to two pages
he had hammered out
a rock-solid deal
on what was to follow.

Touring the Museum of You

Our first display
is the Little Orphan Annie stamp
discovered beside his bed
where the dog is saying ARF
in a bubble over its head.
Then we come to the brightly knitted hat
used in a long winter of chemotherapy.
Several microscopic skin cells
are embedded in the wool.
The last known photograph he took
is of an old Illinois barn
outside Galena in July 1996.
Please don't lean on the glass.
Domestic archaeology
has unearthed a perfect crescent
toenail clipping.
Here we have a gallon of teardrops
lovingly bottled.
This used tube of bronzer
was how he masked
the harsh truth from the world.

Feel free to roam around.

Over

When he saw geese
gathering on a lake in Wisconsin
he said, 'Oh no – summer's almost over.'

Over? It was still hot.
Summer thunderstorms still pounded
nightly on the roof.

Pleeeeeeeeease

Oh for god's sake –
can't we forget it
and you come back to life
and I still travel home
and visit eateries with you in Chicago
and you still blab on about boats and bikes
and we both get on each other's nerves
and you make some pancakes
and then we listen to Prairie Home Companion
and after that a bunch of people arrive
and that annoys me
and you ask me funny questions
and we look at articles and the internet
and you blab on about health
and we get on each other's nerves
and I say let's go down to the beach
and we rent a whacky video
and we make popcorn
and talk on the phone
to all the family – OK?

Sketches for an Elegy

(in memory of my father, Jack O'Callaghan)

Jack and I are resting
under a weeping willow
beside the beach
I want to stop
asking silly questions
and talk about
important topics
such as
which colour he likes best

&

it could ruin
a person's outlook
on a jaunty
August morning
to wake up and hear
the Death March on WFMT
and then see
your ghostly bald father
facing the music
at the table
attempting to eat
a bowl of Cheerios

&

staring from his bed,
he asked, 'How long
did that doctor say?
Was it nine to ten months?
Or was it eight to twelve?'
when I told him six to eight
he shook his head
'Just look at that sky'

&

a cold start to the summer –
everything was haywire
mist all over the skyscrapers
and no customers
down at the beach

୬

we stood in the park
looking for exotic migrating birds
resting on their way north
for the summer
yellow and blue and red birds
everywhere

୬

sitting around
the chemotherapy room
for hours
I read all the magazines – twice
listening to the others
talk about the price of wigs
the great plumber
they had found

୬

Sunday in August
nothing much doing
we go and get groceries
you need a bench to rest on
so we head for the beach
between the skyscrapers
once you feel better
we take off our shoes
and wade in the lake

୬

you pull me over and whisper
'See this guy. I've known him for years
– watch what happens when we pass by'
nothing
'Nobody recognises me any more'

༄

he hears me arranging the flight
'Can't you stay another week?'
how was I supposed to know
he'd have only
three more of his own?

༄

we let you go alone
to pick up
your camera lens downtown
but I worried
the whole time
what if you lost your balance
what if you couldn't walk any further

༄

we're watching David Letterman
and you're paging through
the L.L. Bean summer sale catalogue
you see a shirt you like
and say, 'I won't need it
but one of the boys
could have it'

༄

you lean forward
and I see a big
pillowy thing
protruding from your side
'It's my liver'

              ❧

you have hand spasms
and you can't eat
you can't walk very far
you have no hair
but you can see the sky
the lake
the sunset to the west
so you're OK

              ❧

you scratched your name
into cameras, pens, Swiss Army Knives
you etched your name
into sidewalks, kites, clouds, days

              ❧

the monk eating pasta
in Dubuque Iowa
was the one I needed
to tell me something helpful
or at least not scary
– no use: he didn't have secrets
of the universe
just a plate of vermicelli

              ❧

we were running
around the park
and down to the beach
picking up trash
the slobs
had left behind
hey slobs: no one's left
to pick up your garbage
why not go nuts

&.

some were shocked
some looked away
others didn't recognise you
some got all teary
a few opted for chirpy
the doorman slapped your back
and said you looked great
on the bus
people stood up
to let you sit down

&.

the last entire day
I will ever see you
is Chicago Air Show day
– for godsake
it isn't that often
you're having brunch
on the 22nd floor
and a Stealth Bomber
flies past the window
like a black triangle
from Planet Death

&.

in that story
you're three or four
hanging out in the 1930s
in your Irish grandfather's room
he's sick and depressed
but you want him
to play with you:
you toss the rubber ball
in his direction
– as you're telling me
your voice changes
weeping, you say
'All I wanted
was for him to toss it back.
He wouldn't do it'

&

when someone
can hardly walk
hardly breathe
hardly move
and needs to rest
on a fire hydrant
beside rush hour traffic
you start to panic
trying to figure out
how you'll get him home
a few more blocks

&

the merchandise you ordered
arrived after you had died
we wondered
what it was
you felt you needed
in your last days
we tore it open

like a secret message
that would explain everything
you wanted us to know:
a tall white chef's hat

&.

you tried to scribble
directions down for us nudniks:
taxes, good repairmen,
what to do
if the pipes froze,
how to apply
for a property assessment
pages and pages
on how to live

&.

I wanted to belt
every person
who grabbed your arm
and put on a pitying voice
I wanted to guard you
from anyone shaking their head
dabbing their eyes
they could save their pity
for somebody else

&.

sitting in the children's section
on a little chair
wearing your HANGTIME baseball cap
you page through a whacky book
and nearly forget

&.

there isn't much hope
80% are dead
within 16 months
but he'll try a few things
and see how it goes

෨

driving you to chemotherapy
I realised I couldn't depend
on you any more
my strong father

෨

Miss You-Know-Who
wore skeleton earrings
with light-up red eyes
beneath a black cowboy hat
complementing her silver metallic
baseball jacket and knit mini-skirt
to your Memorial Service
– you would have been proud
of her genius at being insane

෨

my meals boiled down
to microwave bowls and minutes
you would holler
from the bedroom
three minutes for peas
or seven for a potato
five minutes for fish
it didn't matter
gourmet wasn't called for
everything tasted like dirt

෨

you still laughed at Seinfeld
and watered your plants
and read *The New Yorker*
and the Tuesday Science section
OK, it hurt a lot
and you said you'd never wear
your bike helmet again
but dying was easier
than I'd thought

&

when we were pretending you were OK
we planned a trip up the Missouri
like Lewis & Clark
what boat what route what time-frame
we studied *Undaunted Courage* for pointers
it would be great

&

this is a foreign year to you
things will become unfamiliar
inventions you never heard of
gadgets you never used

&

after everything
poison
scars
laser beams of radiation
he says the tumors
are bigger than ever
there is just one more thing
he can try
you asked how it would be
dying – talk me through it
then started painting a picture
of the red barn we saw near the Mississippi

&

early on
when you still had some energy
we went for a spring walk
in Lincoln Park
and saw a man making a reed sculpture
floating on a pond
you wanted to know
how they float
where did he get the reed
would it eventually sink
who commissioned it
what made him want to
create environmental sculpture
you needed to know

&

at the monastery
we each got a room
to think in
you did your thinking
asleep

&

you didn't want to take the white stuff
but I made you do it twice a day
you complained
but you still drank it
how could you live without eating
that's what the white stuff did
it made hunger

&

Jack and me
on fold-up chairs
at the funeral parlour
my cousin's in that coffin

beside the flowers
relatives bending over
to talk to you
eyes everywhere noting
your ghostly appearance

੨ੳ

would you do me
just one favour?
quit sitting like that
quit staring at the sky
don't sit and stare
you aren't the sit-and-stare type
go fix something
get out your tools
get busy and hammer

੨ੳ

I'm blabbing away
about Irish people
you don't know
or houses
you'll never see
forgive me
it's just my way
of being inconsolable

੨ੳ

remember how you told me
your mom used to
stroke your forehead and say,
'there, there' and how that
always made you feel better

੨ੳ

what do I need to say about you
I didn't say before
you let me keep a horse in the city
– now that was nuts right there
you took me on a fossil-hunting expedition
and gave me Navajo earrings

       ਟ

when he was crying
he said, 'I'm not sad.
Just sentimental'

       ਟ

the last page
about that summer
must be on the topic
of beaches
and how you loved them
and the machines which cleaned them
the police patrolling them
little old Russian ladies on the benches
the whackos dancing around on them
in the middle of the night
barges on the horizon
and the pier we walked down
to scatter your ashes

Calligraphy

(1983–2000)

after Sei Shonagon

Calligraphy

I *Reading a Letter*

She has waited
beside her charcoal fire for days
and now receives an answer.

It is a small twig
with two buds
and full pear blossom,

wrapped in the palest
lavender rice paper.
She smiles; smells the blossom.

II *A Meeting*

They lie together
all night whispering
and touching cheeks.
The shutters are open
that face the garden;
they dread the first
bird calls that start
the morning off.

III *A Heian Lady*

The silk she wears
reflects the season.
In daylight she is shy,
hides behind a painted screen.
At night she hates a mosquito

to flutter its wings near her face.
She writes a book kept in a pillow.
It says, 'It is getting so dark
I can scarcely go on writing;
and my brush is all worn out.'

IV *Reincarnation*

I have no willow-green robe now
of Chinese damask.
No layers of unlined robes

in peach-coloured silk.
No gown of Chinese gauze
with blue prints over white.

Where are my jacket of light violet
lined with scarlet
and my plum-red skirt?

Days

I used to spend my days
strumming a *koto*,
arranging fresh blossoms
in a glazed vase,
reciting a poem that begins
'The days and months flow by'
or, with a brush, painting the view.
But my parents
wanted me to go to court
and find a husband.
So now I live
with the other ladies-in-waiting
and never have
a moment to myself.

At Noon in Summer

I wave my fan, but it does no good.
My robes of flowers and gown of blossoms
have wilted and withered.
My hair, a long black shawl,
is damp with perspiration.
No branches stir. The air is thick
with buzzing insects who cool themselves
with tiny jewelled wings.
Just as I am about to dip my hands
in a bowl of iced water, a messenger
wearing a white costume
brings me a note on bright red paper
tied to a deep pink bloom.
Putting down my fan
(which wasn't helping anyway)
I think how much my friend must care
to write on such a suffocating day.

Opals

Lying on my stomach,
silk pillows underneath me,
I trace the outline
of each plum blossom
on my sleeve
and try to hide my face
from the other ladies
with the screen of my hair.
They are discussing the Prince,
gossiping about which royal robe
suits him best.
I have traced the flower six times now,
hoping they won't ask me my opinion
or notice the handful of opal teardrops
decorating my sleeve.

Thinking About Sad Things

I

Not long ago
he picked me for my
cherry lips, my apple cheeks.

But now I see
he prefers peaches and plums
and deep purple grapes.

II

I woke this morning
and ordered my ladies
to sew three new robes
and a Chinese jacket.

I sent someone to pick herbs,
another to buy rare incense.
From a perfumed case I unwrapped
my newly-painted fan.

At nightfall I was ready:
My hair hung like the night sky,
all jewelled and black.
He never came.

The Royal Hair

The Empress is five feet tall
her hair is six feet long
and trails behind her
in processions.

Every morning
I clean out her combs
and prepare perfumed oils
to dress her black strands.

Today she sits on a silk cushion
watching the snow fall.
Her voice is weak – her hair is damp
and I can tell she is drowning in a sea of tears.

The tangles and knots
are as thick as rope
but I don't mind – my hair
is twice as fine and shiny.

Flute

Sitting in Her Majesty's apartment
one evening, I heard a flute outside
and listened as though the music
were for my ears only.

When it stopped playing, the Empress said:
'That flute was like the autumn wind.
Why did you make no answering sound?'
The ladies around her giggled at me.

I replied, 'It was the flute's fault,
it passed too soon
and did not wait for my response.'
'Splendid,' the Empress smiled,
'that's precisely what you should have said.'

Winter

I *Empress Sadako Considers Snow*

When I wore my hair
plain and straight
I loved deep drifts
in my father's yard.
We would spend all day
making a snow mountain,
praying to Goddess Shirayama
not to let it melt.
Now I stir the red embers
in my brazier, watching flurries
through the icy lattice.
No one should disturb
the snow outside my rooms
by shuffling wooden clogs there
or heaping it into a silly mountain.
Snow is shapeliest when left alone.

II *Silver*

I'm the only one who seems to care any more
about the Winter Festival at Kamo.
The evening must be cold enough for snow,
with bonfires, dancers and musicians.
first I hear the sound of drums,
then my eyes follow the light
from the flaming pine torches.
I am always overjoyed at the costumes
of lustrous silk, frozen stiff with ice
and the palace roof outlined in white
seems thatched in silver.
Everyone says, 'You get too excited.'
How can I help it?
I will stay up remembering
until the dawn bell.

III *Men and Precipitation*

My dislike of rain is profound.
Your hair goes stringy,
mud cakes your shoes and hem
and the whole world
becomes a drippy damp
annoyingly stupid place.
But if a man arrives during a storm,
dressed in the yellow-green
of a Chamberlain
or, best of all, in a proper Court robe
moistened by sleet,
I can't hide my admiration.
I forget all about the hateful showers,
organise dry clothes, a warm drink
and pay careful attention
to wringing out his costume.
Nothing pleases me more
than a secret meeting
with a man covered in raindrops.

Yukinari Is Glad

When the parcel of square cakes arrived
I wasn't sure how to reply.
Korenaka suggested I just eat them.
But I took a piece of fine red paper
and wrote a one-sentence note,
attached the usual blossoms
and forgot about the whole thing.

Ten minutes later Yukinari
stood outside my room smiling,
telling me how glad he was
I hadn't sent a poem to him.
'I believe women
who are pleased with themselves
churn out endless poetry,' he added.

I bowed, flapped my fan
and looked at him secretly
out of the corner of my eye
to see if he was serious.
Gaze, flutter, flutter.
He got no pleasure from women
who versified at the drop of a hat.

The Three-Foot Curtain of State

has only the tiniest gap
along the top of its frame.
Luckily that space normally
corresponds to the eye of a man
standing outside the curtain
and the lady inside fanning the air
with her eyelashes.
As long as the couple are
average height and their eyes
speak the same language,
it works perfectly.

Calling Out

a woman's name must be done properly.
During the day a visitor should mumble it
so people won't think he knows
how to pronounce it very well.
But at night that would be wrong.
A gentleman who comes under stars
to visit a lady-in-waiting
must bring a servant with him
who can call out the lady's name.
It's much better to keep the palace
guessing who her admirer might be.

Spring Robe

The most important thing
is to blend the shades of spring
into the layers of your robes.
Forget about brown until autumn.
Concentrate on pink
and you really can't go wrong.
What I feel about patterns
you probably know already:
only the outer robe
should be delicately decorated.
If you can't work out why
I pity you.
It wouldn't take a genius
to see that all your underlayers
are leading up to a magnificent
froth of spectacular peonies
or any other blossom you want.
So long as it takes the breath
from everyone who encounters it.
If it goes unnoticed
it's back to the drawing board,
try a new dyer.
Life is way too short
for blasé colours.
Look at the peach tree.
Learn from the cherry buds.

Lady Norimitsu

The dog
outside my shutters
once was Lady Norimitsu
in figured silk robes.
When we speak to her,
or if she hears us gossip
behind screens,
she barks and yelps.
Her eyes fill with tears
at an unhappy love story
just the way they did
in her former life.

Pilgrim

Thinking my usual
gloomy thoughts one day
it occured to me
that I might make some pilgrimages.
'How frightening!'
was my mother's reaction.
She is a very old-fashioned person.
'What about the thugs
on the road to Ishiyama
and the dangerous way
to Mount Kurama –
wouldn't you be scared?'
she asked me, with her
head in her hands.
I was allowed
only a short retreat
to Kiyomizu Temple.
So when I arrived
I couldn't pray sincerely.

Reply

I know it's uncouth
to blow my own trumpet,
but when the Chancellor himself

says that I write
snappy replies to notes
I get slightly conceited.

It's not just the words –
I choose a piece of thin
and rare red paper,

use the best ink and brush,
then attach the letter
to a sprig of plum blossom.

Each detail
conveys a special message
of its own.

Yawns

The other ladies
have retired
to their rooms
and the watchmen
are half asleep.
I am artistically arranged
under seven layers
of autumn-shaded robes
and an outer jacket
of damask embroidered
with silk leaves.
I wish I could hear
the wooden clunk
of your servant's clogs
on the pebbles outside my shutters.
If you don't come soon
the rice cakes will have gone stale,
my straw mat may be
stencilled on my face
and my perfectly straight hair
will look like I've
seen a ghost.
The temple bell
has struck three
and my yawns
are as numerous
as the stars.

Conundrums

How can such a stupid insect
as a fly be allowed
to put its clammy feet
on anything it lands on?
But what drives me really crazy
is snow shimmering
on the roof of some pathetic shack.
If a moonbeam strikes it
at the same time
I shake my head
and admit
I'll never understand
the world.

Mosquito's Eyelash

I was trying to have a conversation
with the new Captain of the Inner Palace Guards
but Masamitsu wouldn't go away.

When he asked the Captain
his opinion of paintings on fans,
I whispered wispily, 'Don't answer him.

If we ignore him, maybe he'll go.'
'What's that?' the Captain responded,
'Did you say something?'

Masamitsu, on the other hand, screamed,
'Really! If that's how you talk about me,
I'll stay here all day long.'

It is said of Masamitsu
that he could hear the sound
of a mosquito's eyelash falling.

Time

Only a moment ago
he lay beside me
saying silly poetic things.
The mat is still warm,
incense from his robe
haunts the air.

Bright

We sat on the edge of the veranda
raking ashes to keep warm
and to enjoy the snow
turning pale pink at dusk.

When it was dark
the snow was our lamp.
We talked about snowy subjects
until the dawn bell rang.

Imagine our laughter
and we will thaw out
from a thousand years
to live that way again.

Lady Hyobu

as you all know
is a great friend of mine.
But we don't get on
when it comes to calligraphy.
I was practising my characters
in her room last week
when she said to me,
'Would you mind
not using that brush?'
I never say things like that
if she uses my best brush
or keeps asking what's
inside my writing box
or lets the bristles
soak forever in ink
so they're ruined.
Another thing –
it's very annoying
when I'm sitting there
trying to work on a poem
and she gives me a dirty look
and orders me out of her light.

Sleeves

Call me old-fashioned
but this craze
for uneven sleeves
seems idiotic.
In the first place
they unbalance the robe
so it hangs all lopsided
and the woman wearing them
has to keep tugging
to keep her jacket closed in front.

Evenly matched sleeves
are elegant and graceful
so I don't see why
the fashion gurus
make us don these ridiculous creations.
Go ahead and wear wide sleeves
(awkward though they are)
during court ceremonies
but let's at least
keep them symmetrical.

Squeamish

Here is a pretty vulgar topic:
rice starch being mixed with water.
You might need to avert your eyes
because other disgusting things
are those tongs used in fires
during The Festival of the Dead.

There's no use pretending
these items don't exist.
So, whether they are inauspicious or not,
please notice
I'm not squeamish
about mentioning them.

Paper Shortage

Don't make excuses
about how difficult it is
to find a sheet
of delicate red-tinted Chinese
paper.

Send a message
on a flat white pebble
or the stem of a hollyhock.
Etch your words
on a purple lotus petal.

Women with Children Should Keep Them Under Control

I am talking to a woman in my room
who has brought her four year old son,
Matsugimi, for an afternoon visit.
The boy is picking up everything
he can reach and poking anything
he's not tall enough to grab.
'Be quiet, Matsugimi,
the grown-ups are speaking,'
his mother whispers indulgently
when he pushes my most precious comb
into her face and demands
to know what it is.
Then he snatches my good fan
and runs after the cat,
waving it at her tail.
'You naughty child,' she smiles,
patting his melon head,
'you mustn't do that, you'll break the fan.'
I anxiously grit my teeth.

A View of Mount Fuji

(for Patrick Scott)

When Emperor Ichijo
asked me what I wanted
as a parting gift
I answered Mount Fuji.

Towards the end
of the Third Month
a Court Chamberlain
led me to new quarters.

I lit a charcoal fire,
arranged my combs and fans
the way I like them
and took in my surroundings.

The lattice was decorated
with patterns of gold leaf
and as I raised the blind
Mount Fuji waited in the distance.

Here I give you Fuji-san
dressed in imperial robes
so that you will not forget me.
He was mine.

Rumble

The seventh month
begins with a moon celebration.
I love to watch
the Royal Party lit up
by fireflies in the heat.
It might sound eccentric
but I wear my willow-green robe
behind the garden lattice
smelling grass smells,
hearing laughter at the pond,
feeling the silk breeze
touch my hair.
An electric summer night:
distant rumble,
lightning on the horizon.

Summer Storm

My cheek rests on a pillow
facing the Iyo blind.
The back of my neck
is hot and sticky
so sleep is impossible.
I wait for the tiniest breeze,
gaze sideways at the lake,
see the summer storm
on the horizon to the east
as I lie on my cot.
The room shakes with thunder,
lightning flashes in the downpour;
rain lashing the Iyo blind
lands like sacred water
from a temple fountain
on me and on my patterned robe.

Auspicious

All day I've been travelling,
trying to avoid an unlucky direction.
Each way is worse than the one before.
To the northeast: ominous clouds,
facing west: a burning fireball.

I am surrounded by inauspicious noises
– screams, barking dogs, sneezes.
When will I learn
to travel the most auspicious road:
toward the quiet garden?

Two Lines

The gentlemen of the Sixth Rank
must be easily pleased.
They have been over-praising
two lines I scribbled
with an old piece of charcoal
late at night.
It was something about
visiting a grass-thatched hut
and who would bother
with such a lowly place.
But now I hear
how the Court Nobles
have copied it onto their fans!
His Excellency Tadanobu
even came and pounded
on my half-shutters
looking like the hero
from a romance.
The sleeves from his grape jacket
draped over my screen
are the best reward.

New Poems

(2008)

Problems

Take weeds for example.
Like how they will overrun
your garden and your life
if you don't obliterate them.
But forget about weeds
– what about leaves?
Snails use them as handy
bridges to your flowers
and hordes of thuggish slugs
will invade – ever thought about *that*?
We won't even go into
how leaves block up the gutters.
I sure hope you aren't neglecting
any puddles of water in your bathtub
– discoloration will set in.
There is the wasp problem,
the storms problem, the grass
growing-between-the-bricks-in-the-driveway problem.
Then there's the remembering to
lock-all-the-windows problem.
Hey, knuckleheads!
I guess you just don't appreciate
how many problems there are.

The Net

I am the Lost Classmate
being hunted down the superhighways
and byways of infinite cyber-space.
How long can I evade the class committee
searching for my lost self?

I watch the list
of Found Classmates
grow by the month.
Corralled into a hotel ballroom
festooned with 70s paraphernalia,

bombarded with atmospheric
hit tunes, the Captured Classmates
from Sullivan High School
will celebrate thirty years
of freedom from each other.

I peek at the message board:
my locker partner,
out in California, looks forward
to being reunited with
her old school chums.

Wearing a disguise, I calculate
the number of months left
for me to do what I do best,
what I've always done:
slip through the net.

Tumbleweed

Just because
I never mentioned
blue lizards
some might
mistakenly assume
I've never
been to Kentucky.
And just because
I never described
a dead porcupine
on a mountain road
you probably conclude
I've never been
to Colorado.
Wrong.
A glacier in Norway,
a prehistoric village in Orkney,
an Amish town in Indiana,
a genuine plantation house
on Chesapeake Bay
have all been
in my direct line of vision.
Tumbleweed outside Durango?
It rolled right over
my big toe.

Big Feet

The old sister
says to her younger brother:
I thought you'd be on this bus.

She wants to buy him
a pair of snow boots
so he can walk more
and save on the bus fare.
You need to economise.

She is reminiscing
about Oak Park in the 40s
and how she would
plonk him on a bench
while she went ice skating
under the floodlights.

Man did I ever bruise my keister!
They are laughing
about those times.

Her blue nails
clasp her handbag
as she explains
how if he doesn't
get the right size boot
his arches will collapse.
*That's what happens
with big feet.*

Brass Polish

Some topics are easy to think about.
But the topic of you –
that is something I avoid.
How can I have met you?
It doesn't add up.
I get a headache.
I turn my thoughts to plants
visualising which area
of the garden needs
a tall blue flower:
no headache.
You are outside the kitchen
window looking in –
who sent me here?
It is not an off-the-peg life.
Believe me, it's different.
Everything is lethal.
That tall blue flower kills me
and the sky kills me
and what I used to be
and what I will be
and you on the other side
of the table, eating an orange
and reading a review,
you kill me too.
It is not worth thinking about.
I could go nuts.
So I weed the garden path
and put clothes in the washing machine:
sane activities, you'll agree.
But I can't understand any of it.
Maybe you are just a mirage.
Only I see your reflection
on the electric kettle
so you can't be that either.
I crouch down at the mail slot
and use brass polish
to make it as bright as I can.
It is really what I think
on the topic of you.

Old Timer

O flowery perfume
of this new century
you may smell nice
but my nose
prefers twentieth-century flowers.
I'm old-fashioned
about twentieth-century rooms
with twentieth-century people
in them saying outmoded stuff.
No – the future isn't
on my list of must-haves.
I know where my loyalties lie.

Lettergesh Strand

has all these ghosts
running through the
windy spray.
Wave after wave
of people I know
haunting the beach
like translucent jellyfish.
There goes my father
examining a rock pool
with a starfish floating.
I wish a handful of bleached sand
didn't remind me of that
plastic bag labelled
*This package contains
the cremated remains of...*

                    *

The ringing
gets louder.
I search everywhere:
I push aside soft
rounded rocks,
globs of seaweed,
pick up a tiny
curved shell
and hold it
to my ear.
Your voice
– a little distant –
is talking to me,
telling your old jokes,
gushing about
where you are now.
It's great to hear
from you.

I should have known
you'd be hanging out
on this chilly Connemara beach.
No – I'm not in a rush.
Keep talking.
I'm listening.

Brightly Knitted Bolivian Ch'ullu

Jack, my father, I am flying to you
on words,
on white-topped condor wings
of thoughts
to the high altiplano
where you are perched.
I need to tell you
the message hidden in the ch'ullu,
the pasamontana, the brightly knitted hat,
I made for your last winter.

I worked in magic tocapu patterns
and Bolivian pictographs.
It was a spell.
Bright green birds with yellow eyes
against a lavender background
meant *don't leave this world.*
The waves knitted into the band
above your eyes
were talking about
how happy and well
the lake water would make you.

Oh I can't remember what-all
I wished to say in my knitted hieroglyphs.
I clicked those needles furiously
watching Incan markings appear.
I wanted your ch'ullu to have powers.
When you pulled it over your ears
I whispered to you.

Unanswered Questions

why you ate your popcorn
with a tablespoon
the reasoning behind
bowls of ice cream
in the microwave
theories on lake water
how you felt
regarding catalogue purchases
the philosophical argument
behind disfiguring
your new bicycle
thoughts on nutrition
thoughts on vitamins
the nitty-gritty details
of setting up
ceiling movie-screen
projector and sound-system
you in your top hat and tails
the logistics of how you got married
why you aren't alive
why you are here beside me
what happened to your hardware
and tool collection
where your umbrella hat might be

Two Paintings by John Register

Waiting Room for the Beyond

You pull back the curtain
in the examination cubicle
and quit horsing around
when the cancer specialist arrives.
He has some news
which your family
may find difficult to deal with.

Somebody has to take a seat
in the waiting room for the beyond.
So we inspect the accommodation:
green leatherette chair facing
the plate glass windows.
Below you – clouds.
Come here and sit down.

Parking Lot

Oh it's you all right –
I'd recognise those feet
pointing up
from that garden lounger
anywhere.
It must be
where you're at now.
No worries
and a Cadillac.
Gazing out across Lake Michigan
for as long as it takes.
No nutty relatives
to give advice to.
No bill-collectors.
No neighbourhood meetings.
No children demanding
this or that.
Recliner, Sedan de Ville, lake.
Paradise.

Eldorado

In Salamanca, Santiago, Seville
we can behold the gold
of America sparkling
on every church altar,
gilding every angel.
But God does not love that.
God is not impressed
with all that showing off.
He chuckles to himself
at the lopsided, ramshackle
adobe church at Chimayo
with its painted wooden altar.
He sees the dry scrub
of New Mexico
and performs a miracle.
In the side chapel
the floor is mud.
Pilgrims gather a handful
of holy soil for hope.
No matter how much
golden earth they mine
there is an infinite reserve.

Bad Cells

You sit in the Cancer Chapel
wedged somewhere between
the health food store
and the knick-knack emporium
praying.

For you there is no
such time as Saturday afternoon.
No such place as
the upper level
of a cheesy shopping centre.

It is hard work
shopping for life.
Soup selections, fashion trends
fall away until all
that's left is you

in a dingy retail unit
pretending it's a chapel,
while you concentrate
on begging for bad cells
to be made good.

Tell Me This is Normal

Tell me the roaring noise
and the metallic grinding
and the engine blast
and the shivering and shuddering
and sliding and listing
not to mention the way it feels
like we are sinking
and how it seems as if
we are in big big trouble
– tell me this is normal
for an autumn cruise
down Killary Harbour.
Until I hear you confirm
this is a normal situation
I will remain
in the following position:
white-knuckled fist
gripping edge of table
heart pounding
mouth open in grizzly grimace
look of terror on face
body rigid and braced
for imminent disaster...
If at all possible
tell me this is normal
pretty darn soon
so I can start enjoying
the scenery here
in murky old Connemara.

Scary

Journeys can be frightening
wouldn't you say?
When everyone on the plane
stops talking and grabs the arm rest
and you're over the North Atlantic,
what about that scenario?

Parties – scary.
Bosses – scary.
Reviews – scary.
Families – very scary.
Computers – scary.
Waiters and waitpersons – scary.

It is all so complicated to explain –
like the way my father used to ask me,
'How did you get to be so scared?'
Try being born, like me,
on Kafka's birthday
and you wouldn't need to ask.
People are terrifying, for one thing.
No way around
that sad and sorry fact.
Mr Hotshot is in a hurry
and happens to run you over ('by mistake').
Or if you're out strolling along
and somebody gets a yen
to stab somebody
then sees you?
I find that a little scary.

Houses – hope the foundation isn't faulty.
Water – hope it isn't sewage-laden.
Buses – hope the driver quits talking on his cell phone.
Diet Coke – hope those chemicals are OK.
Work – hope you don't get a nervous breakdown.
Aches – hope it isn't a tumour.

Hey, parents – do you worry yourself sick
whatwith sharp edges and open flames
and bullies and learning disabilities
and maniacs and drugs?
Scary.

Getting old – scary.
Money – scary.
The future – scary.
Burglars – scary.
Superbugs – scary.

Let's welcome in the New Year
hiding under the bed
with a baseball bat.
Scary.